Three Jovial Huntsmen

THREE JOVIAL HUNTSMEN
adapted and illustrated by Susan Jeffers

The text of this book is set in 20 pt. Bembo. The illustrations are pen and ink drawings, with wash overlays painted in red, yellow, blue and black oils, reproduced in four-color halftone and line.

for M.P.T.

There were three jovial huntsmen,
As I have heard men say,

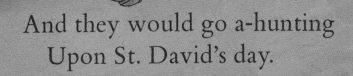

And they would go a-hunting
Upon St. David's day.

All the day they hunted,
And nothing could they find,

But a ship a-sailing,
A-sailing with the wind.

One said it was a ship,
  The other he said, Nay,
The third said it was a house
  With the chimney blown away.

And all the night they hunted,
   And nothing could they find,
But the moon a-gliding,
   A-gliding with the wind.

One said it was the moon,
The other he said, Nay,
The third said it was a cheese
With half of it cut away.

And all the day they hunted,
  And nothing could they find,
But a hedgehog in a bramble bush,

And that they left behind.

The first said it was a hedgehog,
The second he said, Nay,
The third said it was a pincushion
With the pins stuck in wrong way.

And all the night they hunted,
      And nothing could they find,
But a hare in a turnip field,

And that they left behind.

There were three jovial huntsmen,
    As I have heard men say,
And they would go a-hunting
    Upon St. David's day.

SusanJeffers, a young painter, book designer and illustrator, has drawn the pictures for several children's books, among them Joseph Jacobs' *The Buried Moon*. Ms. Jeffers lives in a cottage in Croton-on-Hudson, N.Y., where she is surrounded by woods and animals.